She Sells Sea Shells

Illustrated by Bruno Merz

ISBN 978-0-9855719-2-4
Printed in Mexico on FSC® paper
from well-managed forests

©2013 Music Together LLC. All rights reserved.
"She Sells Sea Shells" by Kenneth K. Guilmartin
(Music Together LLC/ASCAP), inspired by a traditional
tongue-twister. Music Together is a registered trademark.

Music Together LLC
66 Witherspoon Street
Princeton NJ 08542
www.musictogether.com
(800) 728-2692

MUSIC TOGETHER®

She Sells Sea Shells

Welcome 4
Story 8
Activities 28
Music Page 30
Getting the Music 31

Welcome!

Since 1987, Music Together has been bringing the Joy of Family Music® to young children and their families. This Singalong Storybook offers a new way to enjoy one of our best-loved Music Together songs. We invite you to sing it, read it, and use it as a starting point for conversation and imaginative play with your child.

Using the Book

If you're a Music Together family, you might start singing as soon as you turn the pages. But even if you've never attended one of our classes, you and your child can appreciate our Singalong Storybooks. The illustrations in each book suggest the mood of the song that inspired it, whether playful, mysterious, or soothing. Read the story with your child, and then try some of the suggested activities that follow. Use the book to inspire artwork or enhance pre-literacy skills. You can even invent your own variations of the story or involve the whole family in some musical dramatic play.

Using the Recording Of course, you will want to have a recording of the song to fully enjoy this book. (See page 31 for how to find Music Together CDs, downloads, and videos about using the books.) And if you play an instrument such as piano or guitar, you'll also find it easy to pick out the song using the music page at the end of the book.

About Music Together®

Music Together classes offer a wide range of activities that are designed to be engaging and enjoyable for children from birth through age seven. By presenting a rich tonal and rhythmic mix as well as a variety of musical styles, Music Together provides children with a depth of experience that stimulates and supports their growing music skills and understanding.

Developed by Founder/Director Kenneth K. Guilmartin and his coauthor, Director of Research Lili M. Levinowitz, Ph.D., Music Together is built on the idea that all children are musical, that their parents and caregivers are a vital part of their music learning, and that their natural music abilities will flower and flourish when they are provided with a sufficiently rich learning environment.

And it's fun! Our proven methods not only help children learn to embrace and express their natural musicality—they often help their grateful grownups recapture a love of music, too. In Music Together classes all over the world, children and their families learn that music can happen anywhere, every day, at any time of the day—and they learn they can make it themselves.

Known worldwide for our mixed-age family classes, we have also adapted our curriculum to suit the needs of infants, older children, and children in school settings such as preschools, kindergartens, and early elementary grades. Visit www.musictogether.com to see video clips of Music Together classes; read about the research behind the program; purchase instruments, CDs, and books; and find a class near you. Keep singing!

About the Song

The song "She Sells Sea Shells" is based on a well-known tongue-twister that was originally written about a woman named Mary Anning, born in 1799. The "shells" that Mary sold were actually fossils—often called "curiosities"—that she collected along the coastal cliffs of Lyme Regis, England. Though unschooled, Mary was sought out and respected by eminent scientists and made several important paleontological finds before her death in 1847.

Our song is inspired by a different kind of "curiosity"—the shells of many colors, shapes, and sizes left by the creatures of the sea. These remnants may not be as old as fossils but they, too, are a glimpse into a different world. Children love to sing this song, perhaps because the soothing and mysterious melody hints at the sense of wonder we feel at finding these treasures on the most ordinary of beaches. Try singing it as a round with another adult or an older child (see page 30).

8

She sells sea shells by the seashore.

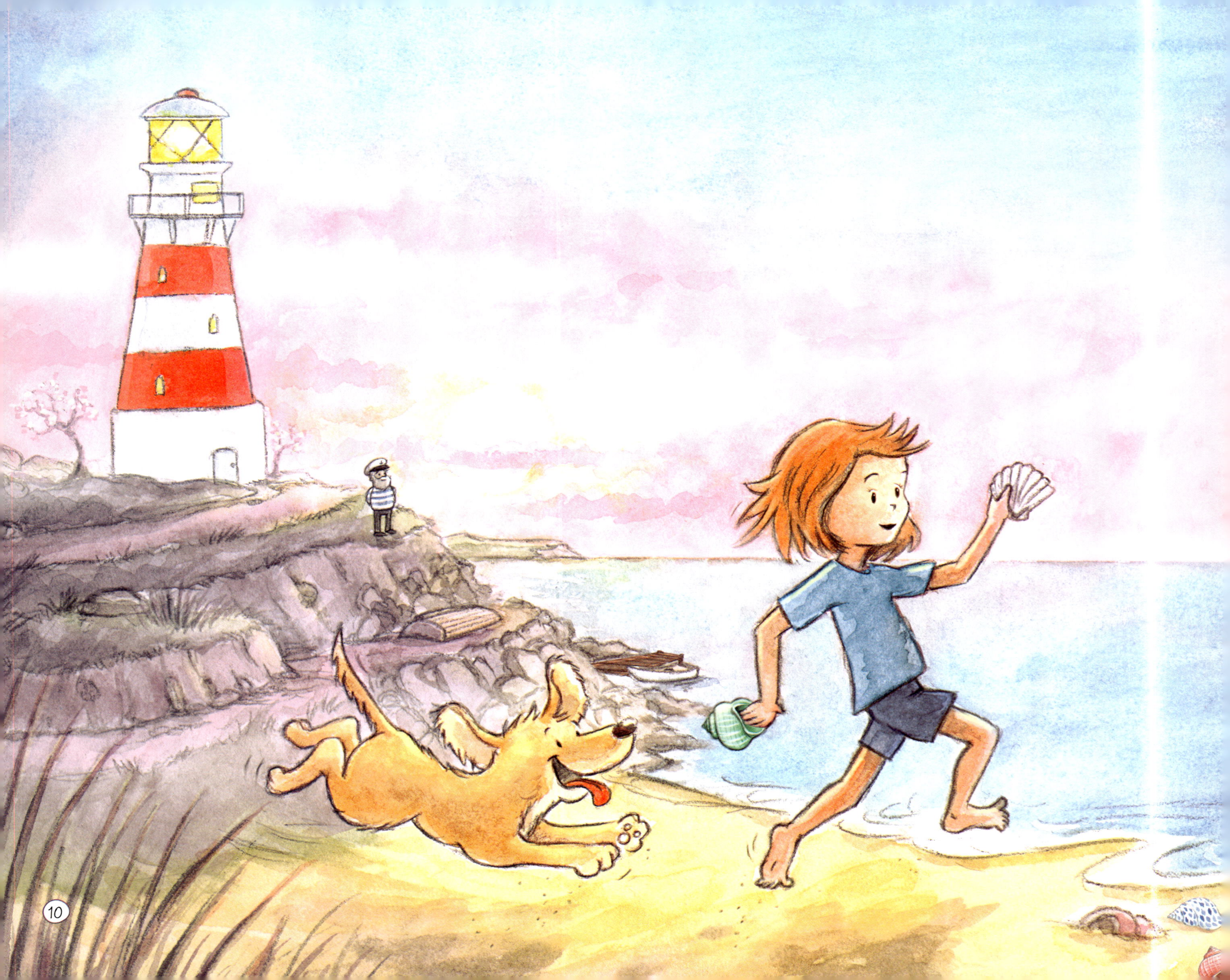

She sells sea shells by the seashore.

Brown and gray and blue,
yellow, pink,
white, green.

Brown and gray and blue, yellow, pink, white, green.

Birds in the sky

Singing songs, flying high while...

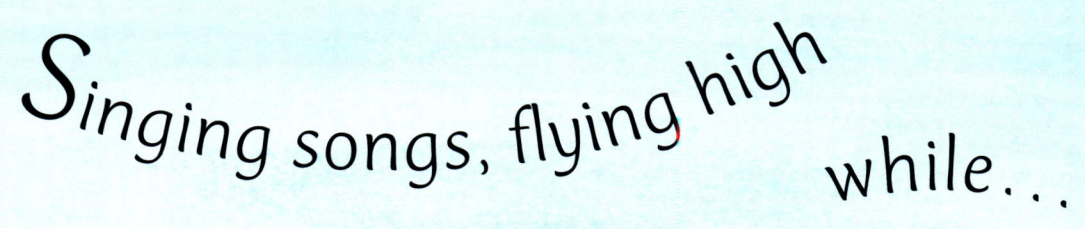

She sells sea shells by the seashore.

She sells sea shells by the seashore.

Oyster, mussel, snail, periwinkle, clam.

Oyster, mussel, snail, periwinkle, clam.

Birds in the sky

Singing songs, flying high while...

She sells sea shells by the seashore.

She sells sea shells by the seashore.

24

She sells sea shells by the seashore.

26

She sells sea shells by the seashore.

Activities

Shells

The shells the girl carries on her tray are in the same order as in the song: "oyster, mussel, snail, periwinkle, clam." Look at the shells with your child and compare them to shells or other things you may have found.

Colors

Look at the shells the girl is collecting. As you sing or read the song, invite your child to find and point to the "brown and gray and blue, yellow, pink, white, green" shells that are shown on the page.

Friends

Keep an eye out for some seaside friends who pop up throughout the story, such as the sand crab, the fish, and the starfish. Have fun finding them and pointing them out.

Literacy

For a pre-literacy activity, older children may enjoy discovering all the S's in the phrase "she sells sea shells by the seashore." Invite your child to point them out as you sing or read the words.

Our World

Notice the different kinds of boats on the water: the girl's rowboat, the sailboats, the small ship—even an ocean liner! Which kind of boat does your child like? Where would he go on it?

At the Beach

Next time you're at the beach with your child, sing this song as you look for shells. Can you recognize any from the pictures in the book?

She Sells Sea Shells

K. Guilmartin (inspired by a traditional tongue twister)

Gently

① She sells sea shells by the sea-shore. She sells sea shells by the sea-shore. ② Brown and gray and blue, yel-low, pink, white, green.
(*alternate verse.* Oys-ter, mus-sel, snail, per-i-win-kle, clam.

Brown and gray and blue, yel-low, pink, white, green. ③ Birds in the
Oys-ter, mus-sel, snail, per-i-win-kle, clam.)

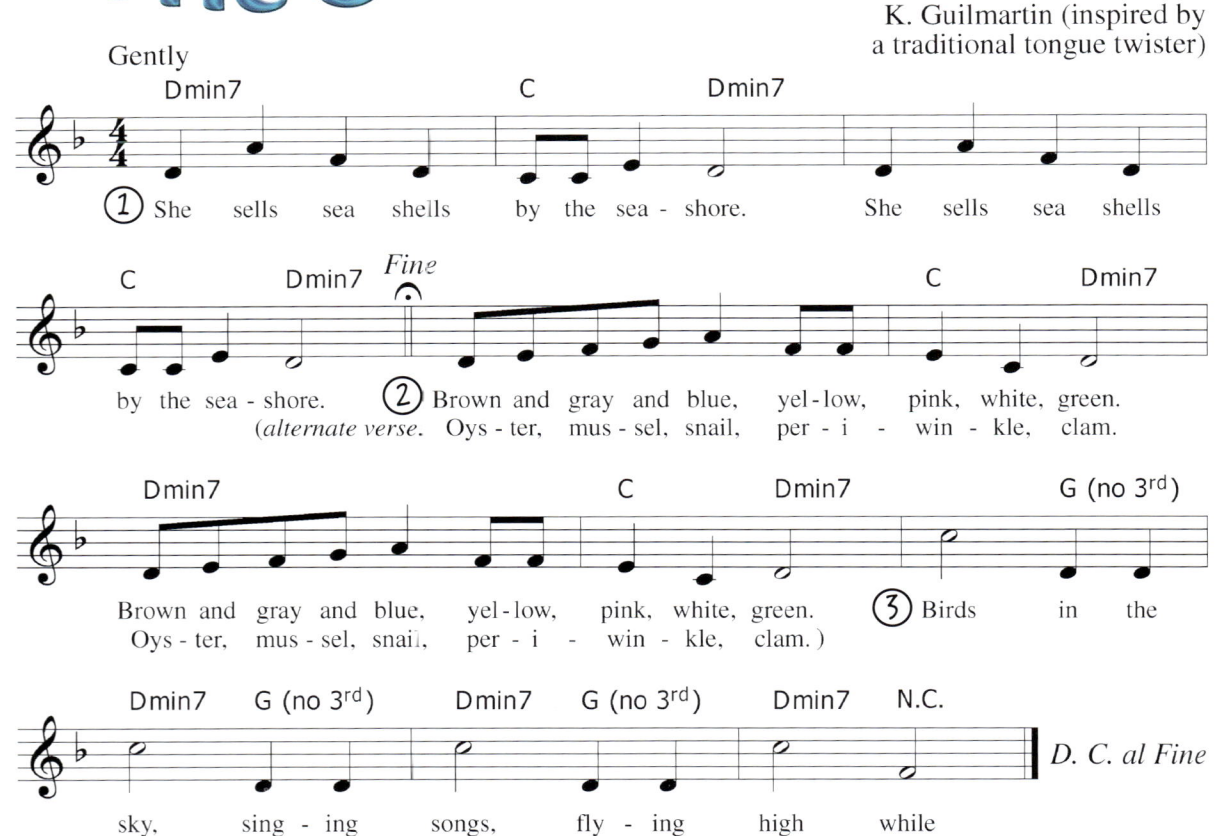

sky, sing-ing songs, fly-ing high while

D. C. al Fine

The melody has three parts — ①②③. They can be sung one by one, all together, or in a round. Try it!

Getting the Music

"She Sells Sea Shells" has been sung in Music Together classes around the world. It can be found on our award-winning Music Together **Family Favorites**® CD—available on our website and in select stores and catalogues—and in the Music Together **Drum Song Collection** for enrolled families. This song and others are also available for download on our website and on iTunes. To get the most out of your Singalong Storybooks, see the videos on our website.

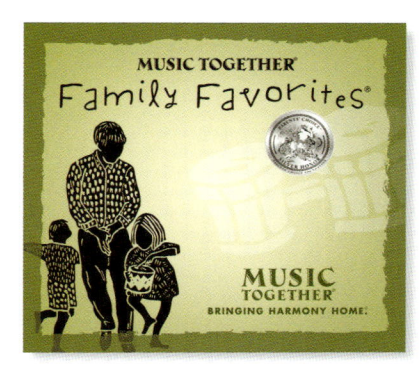

The Family Favorites CD includes 19 songs and a 32-page booklet with many family activities to enjoy. Our award-winning **Family Favorites**® **Songbook for Teachers** features techniques and activities to suit a variety of classroom settings.

Please visit us at **www.musictogether.com**.

Music Together LLC

Kenneth K. Guilmartin, Founder/Director

Catherine Judd Hirsch, Director of Publishing and Marketing

Marcel Chouteau, Manager of Production and Distribution

Jill Bronson, Manager of Retail and Market Research

Susan Pujdak Hoffman, Senior Editor

Developed by Q2A/Bill Smith, New York, NY